CHARLIE NEWCOMER

CHARLIE NEWCOMER

WILBUR B. STOVER

ISBN: 978-93-5614-699-0

Published: 1894

LECTOR HOUSE LLP
E-MAIL: info@lectorhouse.com

CHARLIE NEWCOMER

BY

WILBUR B. STOVER

1894

PREFACE.

I knew Charlie Newcomer, and I loved him. To me he seemed to have a bright future. And that other children may be led to take his good example in uniting with the church while they are yet children, I take pleasure in telling the story of his life. I have told that story often from the pulpit, in children's meetings, and I tell it now, in this way that a larger congregation may be reached.

In the home of Charlie and Bessie's parents at Ringgold, I wrote every word of this sketch. It is with considerable hesitancy, too, that the parents allow the facts to be told, since it enters right into their home life, and since some might misjudge their intention concerning their children.

May his heart's desire now be realized—to be a missionary.

W. B. S.

Edgemont, Md., Feb. 2, 1894.

CONTENTS

Chapter   *Page*

PREFACE. v

I. AT THE RINGGOLD SCHOOL. 1

II. A SUNDAY AT WELTY'S CHURCH. 5

III. TRYING TO FIND SOMETHING. 8

IV. QUESTIONS AND ANSWERS. 11

V. A CHILD OF GOD. 14

VI. A SATURDAY AT HOME. 18

VII. CHARLIE'S LAST DAYS. 20

VIII. BESSIE. 23

CHARLIE NEWCOMER

CHAPTER I.

AT THE RINGGOLD SCHOOL.

"Hurry up Charlie, for as soon as we get our dinner over, we want to play base-ball, and you're on our side, you know," called one of the scholars of the Ringgold school to Charlie Newcomer, as he was going home at noon for his dinner. Charlie's home was only a few rods from the school house, and on the same side of the road.

"All right, boys, I will," he answered in return, and in a minute more he was home.

Dinner was not ready when he reached home, for his mamma had been putting out her washing that forenoon. So he brought the water and then went to the cellar for the bread and butter while his mamma made the gravy, and dinner was soon on the table. While they were eating, Charlie said, "Do you think, mamma, I can get up head this afternoon? I've studied my lessons very well."

"I don't know, indeed," said his mamma, "you cannot unless some one above you should make a mistake, and the other scholars are as anxious to stand well as you are."

"They're awful hard lessons, and surely some one will miss, and I'm just waiting for a chance like that. You know I hate to be foot," he continued, "and if I hadn't 'a' missed that day three weeks ago, I would have been head now."

He had finished his dinner before his mother and little sister, and was off to school while they were yet at the table.

The boys in the play ground had changed their minds about playing base-ball, from the fact that some wanted to begin playing right away, while others wanted to wait for the return of those who had gone home for dinner. Some wanted to choose new sides, and others wanted to remain as they had been the day before; and yet others, as they said, "didn't want to play anyhow," and in the midst of so many voices, they all went to playing "Drop the handkerchief," girls and boys together. Charlie was especially fond of playing "Drop the handkerchief," and when he saw it was that game instead of ball, it did not take long until he was at it with all his might. Adding his kerchief to those already afloat, he ran around the large circle never faster.

Grown up people sometimes wonder how it is that children are willing to play until they are all in a perspiration, but children just as well wonder at grown up people for working with the same result.

The ringing of the school bell brought the game to a close. Nearly all of the scholars went at once into the house, while a few lingered on the porch to get a drink of water and cool off a little before going in.

How quiet it seems just after all the boys and girls are called from the playground to their books.

The school building at Ringgold is at one end of the town, and the town is a little, long one, right on the top of a large, long hill. On either side you can see the mountains, and from Ringgold to the mountain eastward, even away up on the side of the mountain, are thousands and thousands of peach trees.

Within the school house is work. Class after class is called up to recite, and in some of them not many changes are made as to the standing of the pupils. In most of the classes the method of trapping is used. Whenever any one mis-spells a word or makes a mistake on a problem, the next one below him has a chance at it; if he misses, the next has a chance, and so on until the one is found who can make right the error, then that one traps and goes up above all who have missed.

Ever since Charlie had been absent that one day, he had been working especially hard to win his accustomed place at the head of his classes, for whoever missed a day had to "go foot."

That afternoon because the lessons were rather difficult, he hoped to get near to his old place, if not to reach it altogether. When the first class was called, his heart beat just a little faster than while he was preparing his lesson. As he arose from his seat to go, he breathed a little prayer to God, that he might remember well what he had just been learning.

Several problems were missed and as many times somebody trapped up. But not every problem that others had mistaken reached Charlie. One time he thought he would now trap three, when he himself missed, and another got it. In trapping, however, the close of the recitation found him "third" but not "first." And so the class was dismissed for that day.

The last in the afternoon was the spelling class. The teacher frequently began to pronounce the words on the lower part of the page first. "Tournament" was the first word to-day. The next was "constitute." "Coadjutor" was Charlie's first word to spell. "Inaugurate" was mis-spelled near the foot of the class. "Sumac" was missed, and the scholars below were eager. "Ducat" enabled the one above Charlie to trap two. "Joust" was spelled correctly. "Oolite" and "vocable" were missed several times. The lesson was almost closed.

"Compass," said the teacher.

"Fortnight."

"Revolt." That was Charlie's.

"Caoutchouc."

THE RINGGOLD SCHOOLHOUSE.

"C-a-o-u-t-c-h—c-h—can't spell it," said the little man next below Charlie.

"Next," said the teacher.

"C-a-o-u-t-c-h-o-u-c-e."

"Next."

"C-o-o-c-h-o-o—o-o—."

"Next."

"C-h-o-o—"

"Next," and Charlie began to wish he had been foot now, so he could get up more than one at a time.

"K-a-u-o-t-c-h."

"Next," and all eyes began to look toward the head of the class, for the unfortunate word was sure to go there.

"Caoutchouc," again pronounced the teacher, clearly. The bright little girl at the head of the class was a good speller, but hearing so many efforts, she became confused with the word, and although spelling slowly at it, she missed it.

"Next."

"Caoutchouc, is it, teacher?"

"Yes, sir."

"C-o-u-t-c-h-o-u-c."

"Next."

"C-o-u-t-c-h-a-o-u-c."

"Next," and every kind of a way was given to spell that word. It passed on down the class to Charlie. He was waiting, not a little anxiously for it.

"C-a-o-u-t-c-h-o-u-c caoutchouc," and he marched up head with a smile that showed gladness for himself, and love for those in the class at the head of which he now stood.

Some words more and the lesson was recited.

"Charlie," said Earl Rinehart after the bell rang, and they were passing out of the door, "I was glad you got that word right."

"Why so, Earl?"

"Because I'd rather have you head than any one else, even if I do have to be second or third."

And having crossed over the stile, five of them joined in a row and ran a foot-race down the little hill, past Bell's and Newcomer's, on down the road,—save one, who turned off to the right quickly and hurried into the house to tell his mamma of his good fortune in the spelling class.

CHAPTER II.

A SUNDAY AT WELTY'S CHURCH.

The sun was shining brightly on Sunday morning, and all was still and quiet in Ringgold and the country round about. Charlie had buttoned his sister Bessie's shoes, and they both were now sitting on the back porch of their home, talking.

Their papa was in the front room reviewing his Sunday school lesson, and their mamma was re-arranging some things in the kitchen. It was not time to go yet, but the carriage was standing at the gate and the horse was in the stable, harnessed.

"Bessie," said Charlie, "don't you wish you were going to be baptized to-day!"

"Why, Charlie, you know I'm too little," said Bessie.

"How old do you think you ought to be first, anyhow!"

"Oh, I don't know."

"I was just thinking about how nice everything is this morning, and I wonder how it was in the garden of Eden."

"Children, are you ready for Sunday school? Papa is hitching up."

"All right, mamma, we're coming," they answered, and were off together very soon.

On the way to church, no one had much to say. Charlie was sitting on the front seat with his papa, and he was the driver too, while Bessie and mamma sat on the second seat.

The church is down in the valley between the long Ringgold hill and the mountain to the east, and by the time they reached it, several other carriages were already there. The superintendent of the Sunday school had just gotten there a short time before, and all who were there were gathering in to spend a little while in singing before time for Sunday school to begin. The first hymn they sang that morning was

> "Jesus, when he left the sky,
> And for sinners came to die,
> In his mercy passed not by
> Little ones like me."

and all the other verses.

WELTY'S MEETING-HOUSE.

After they sang them they all kneeled down and the superintendent led in an earnest prayer. Then they read the lesson, verse about, and the teachers began work with their classes.

Grown-up people sometimes think the Sunday school is just for the children, and even here at Welty's there were some who seemed to think that way, and the Sunday school consisted mostly of children.

Charlie's teacher took his class to the one end of the church, into an adjoining room, where they could learn so much better, not being annoyed at all by the talking of the other classes. Here in this little room, teacher and class regularly study the Word of God for a half hour every Sunday.

A half hour seems but a short time, and indeed it is, but that is only the recitation period, and that is long enough for such as have studied the lesson well. It takes a good while to tell what we don't know, but not very long to tell what we do know.

Sunday school was over and five minutes later church services began. Nearly all the scholars remained for church. Several ministers were there, and the one who preached talked about the love of God for everybody. He said God loved boys and girls as well as men and women. He loved bad people and good people. He even loved heathen people, and He wants every one everywhere to love Him in return. He said God wants all of us to serve Him, and if we do not serve Him, we can not love Him. He said, too, that the more we serve Him, the happier we are, and the less we do for Him, the more unhappy we are.

He talked about prayer, too. He said some Christians pray and some Christians do not, and how that the best Christians always pray the most.

The preacher was an old man whose beard was already gray with the labors of many years, and everybody said it was a good sermon.

After the meeting there was no haste to go home. Every one seemed desirous of staying there and shaking hands and talking a while. The superintendent nearly always tried to get several to accompany him home, so that they might spend the afternoon together. All the members of that church did in the same way. The children were out on the grass talking with each other and waiting until parents and friends were ready to start for home.

Charlie was among the last to leave, and as he and his papa walked out to the carriage, where mamma and Bessie were waiting for them, he said, "I don't know why I like church so well, papa, I just wish it would last all day."

His papa said, "Before you could walk we always took you with us to preaching." "I'm glad you did," answered Charlie, as he ran to untie the horse before his papa was quite there.

CHAPTER III.

TRYING TO FIND SOMETHING.

One day a little fellow was seen walking back and forth on the road from the store to his home, looking serious, and with eyes close upon the ground. A wagon going by, the man called out, "Charlie, what are you doing?"

"Oh, I lost something, and I'm just trying to find it."

And he kept hunting a long while between his home and the store to find whatever it was he had lost. His mamma had sent him to the store to get some groceries for her. He received the change into his hand, a nickel, and coming home he lost it. His mamma thought he could not find it, but he continued seeking until he did.

"Mamma, I found it," he came in saying, "I knew I could. You thought I couldn't, now you might give it to me." His mamma laughed and then asked him to bring in some water. After he had set the bucket of water on the table he said, "What do you think I was thinking about when I was hunting for that five cents?"

"I can't tell, son."

"Well, mamma," he said, "I would like to be a Christian, can't I? I would like to be baptized soon."

His mamma always prayed that her children might grow in grace as they grow in years, but this was unexpected. She answered: "I am glad you think about that, Charlie, but you are too young now."

"How old must one be first?"

"Well, that varies a good deal, I know."

"I'm *nine* years old."

"Yes, I know."

"Ain't nine old enough?"

"But you must think about it more, Charlie."

"More! I've been thinking about it a long time a'ready."

"Well I'll talk to papa about it, and we'll see what he says. You know we want you always to do right," said his mamma, and he got his magnet, and put pins together and magnetized a needle, and made it swim, and point north and south.

That night after both children were asleep, their parents talked a good deal about what Charlie had said.

"Charlie wants to unite with the church."

"He does? When did he say so?"

"Just to-day, and he is in deep earnest about it, too. I don't know what to think, hardly."

"I hardly think he realizes fully, what he wants to do."

"Poor little fellow, what do you think I had better tell him?"

"I don't know. Suppose he should come and then not hold out. You see that would be bad."

"Yes, and then, papa, what wrong has he done?"

"That's so."

"But you remember four years ago when a certain lady was here on a visit, how she happened to express her unbelief in God. No one thought the children heard a word of it. Charlie was gone in a moment, we thought to play, when he brought in the Bible and laid it on her lap and said, 'Read that, it will tell you what to do.' I always did think Charlie would be a Christian very early in life."

"Yes, I am glad for it, too,—but I guess we'd better wait a while anyhow, and see if he really wants to come," said his papa, and the matter was dropped, and other things were talked about.

Several days passed by till the subject was brought up again. Then Charlie said:

"Nine years; old enough to go to school, old enough to do work, old enough to do good or bad, and not old enough to be baptized. Mamma, I do wish I could."

"Charlie, you never did anything bad."

"Must I do something bad before I can join the church?"

"No, no, but you're so young, you don't need to yet."

"Well, I can't see—" he said, and then, with tears in his eyes, he took Bessie by the hand, and went down across the lot to the old apple tree, where they had a swing and spent often many happy hours.

In a day or two after that, Charlie mentioned at the table, his desire to be a child of God. "I am sure I would hold out," he said, "and if I couldn't I'd be just where I am now. But I could, for Jesus helps, don't He?"

Then nothing more was said for several months about his becoming a child of God. It seemed as if he had forgotten his desire to find something of heaven so young.

The summer was over. All the peaches on the side of the mountain and in the valley had been gathered. The leaves of the trees were yellow and golden, and many had already found their resting place upon the ground. Charlie and Bessie had both been going to school for six weeks already. It was Saturday. There was to be preaching at Welty's that day, and a love-feast in the evening. Charlie had been thinking about the thirteenth chapter of John and the fifteenth, and when all were about ready to go to the meeting he said, "Now, if you had let me join the church last summer, when I wanted to, I could have enjoyed this meeting."

"Why, my dear boy," said his mamma, "you can enjoy it anyhow, can't you?"

"No," said he, "not as I'd like to."

And they all four got into the carriage and started off to the meeting, not saying very much.

CHAPTER IV.
QUESTIONS AND ANSWERS.

Services continued longer one Sunday than usual, and after the meeting was over quite a number of those who had come a distance, upon invitation, decided to stop with others who were not so far from home. Two carriages drove over to the big spring. The Newcomers went with the Sunday school superintendent, and others went elsewhere.

This manner of visiting after the meeting on Sunday, is sometimes a good thing and sometimes it is not. It is good if the occasion is used for the spiritual benefit of those concerned. Sunday is the Lord's day.

In the afternoon, at the superintendent's house, the conversation drifted about on the various phases of religious life, church work, Bible study, educational work, the conversion of children, missionary work, books, papers, and present day life.

The little folks were out somewhere, engaging themselves as they saw proper. Sometimes they came into the room and remained a short time, then out they would go all together.

Charlie remained, however. There may have been *two* boys who preferred to stay in the house.

Toward evening Charlie came to one of those who had been talking with the rest, and leaning over on his knee, he wanted to ask some questions. He had been hearing and not saying anything, and now he wanted some things explained.

"Tell me," he said, "how old is old enough to join the church."

"That varies, Charlie, according to the intelligence and teaching of the child. Some are more fit when they are ten years, than others at twenty."

"Well, but, am I old enough?"

"I think so, don't you?"

"Yes, I do, but another thing. Does an education make a person good?"

"No, it will make you better if you are good, but if a bad man gets education, that doesn't make him good."

"Then is it any use to study so hard to get a good education?"

"Why certainly."

"Tell me."

"Education, Charlie, is just development. You know what development means?"

"Yes sir."

"Well, development gives strength."

"You have noticed that large tree out in the orchard. It was only a chestnut once, but now it is developed. That tree is only an educated chestnut. Which is stronger,—the chestnut tree or the little chestnut?"

"The tree, of course," said he, "but I heard some one say, I think it was just last Sunday, that education spoils some people."

"The right kind of an education will never spoil any one."

"I'm going to get a good education. Papa and mamma said they'd help me, but I want to earn the money myself, and then go a long time."

"And then you'll be a missionary won't you?"

"Could I?"

"You can if you choose."

"What must I do?"

"You must be a good Christian at home, and do all you can for Jesus now. Whoever is not good at home is the same away from home. Do things so people will all love you. If your associates and acquaintances do not love you, it is not likely the heathen will, and love is a great deal of the missionary's preparation. And give. If you have not much, give a little, and if you have more, give proportionately. But it is not all in giving. There is more even in living for the Lord, and just letting one's self be all His."

Charlie seemed to be thinking of something else then, and he spoke out in earnest:

"Doesn't the Bible say we ought to send missionaries everywhere in the world?"

"It says we must '*Go*', yes."

"Were there heathen fifty years ago?"

"Yes."

"Well, then why didn't we send lots of missionaries fifty years ago? I wish I could go."

"Do you want to know, Charlie, how you can tell if you can be a missionary when you are a man?"

"Yes sir," said Charlie.

"Be a little missionary now. Be a Christian. Get new scholars to come to Sunday school. Live for other people all you can. One little person quit eating candy, and gave the money for the Lord, another bought a dozen eggs and raised chickens and sold them for the Lord. A little farmer boy raised potatoes on a little corner of land his papa said he could have, and then sold them for missionary money, and there are many other ways."

"Oh, I know, I know what I'll do!" said several at once. "I'm so thirsty."

"So am I." "No, wait." "Come on."

"We can all do something, then, can't we? I'm dry too."

And the one who was answering questions, together with for six little people, who had gathered around him, went out under the grape arbor, and down by the row of evergreens to the spring, and they all drank heartily from the old tin cup.

An hour later all the visitors had their faces turned toward home, and the children were thinking about being little missionaries at home.

CHAPTER V.

A CHILD OF GOD.

A good many months had passed since Charlie lost the nickel between the store and his home. He had often spoken about his desire to be a real Christian. He was going to school every day, and had more than the average of school-boy-liveliness.

Several years had passed since he and one of the little Sunday school girls swinging in the shade of the old apple tree, had each promised the other to begin to be a Christian while they were young in years. The little girl was first to fulfil her promise, and was now an active little member of the church, praising God by her daily life. He thought more of her for her decision, but he himself was not yet a member of the church, and was already twelve years old.

Brother Early had been preaching every night in Waynesboro for several weeks. A good many people, who lived not too far away from Waynesboro, often drove in to attend the meetings. Charlie was usually on hand, an attentive listener.

On the way home one Sunday night Charlie broke the monotonous rumble of the carriage by asking, "Mamma, do you think I'd be·saved if I'd die?"

And his mamma answered, "Well Charlie, indeed I don't know what to tell you," and no one said anything further for a moment, which seemed ever so long.

"What do you say about it, papa?" continued Charlie in a very earnest, pleading tone of voice.

"You have asked a pretty hard question," said his papa. "Just at this time of your life we cannot know. God is just, and may be you'd be saved—may be not." After several minutes, which seemed almost like hours, as the carriage moved slowly up the hill, his mamma, ever anxious about her boy, as all mammas are, said, "Why do you ask such questions, Charlie?"

"Well, mamma," he answered, "I can't stand it any longer. My heart pretty near breaks when we are at meeting. I do wish I could join the church."

Now, his parents had talked the matter all over by themselves, and they had decided to allow Charlie to come at this time, if he really wanted to, and they would also encourage their son. When he had thus spoken, they told him the words that his boyish heart had been aching to hear for already so long a time, that he should "come now," if he wished.

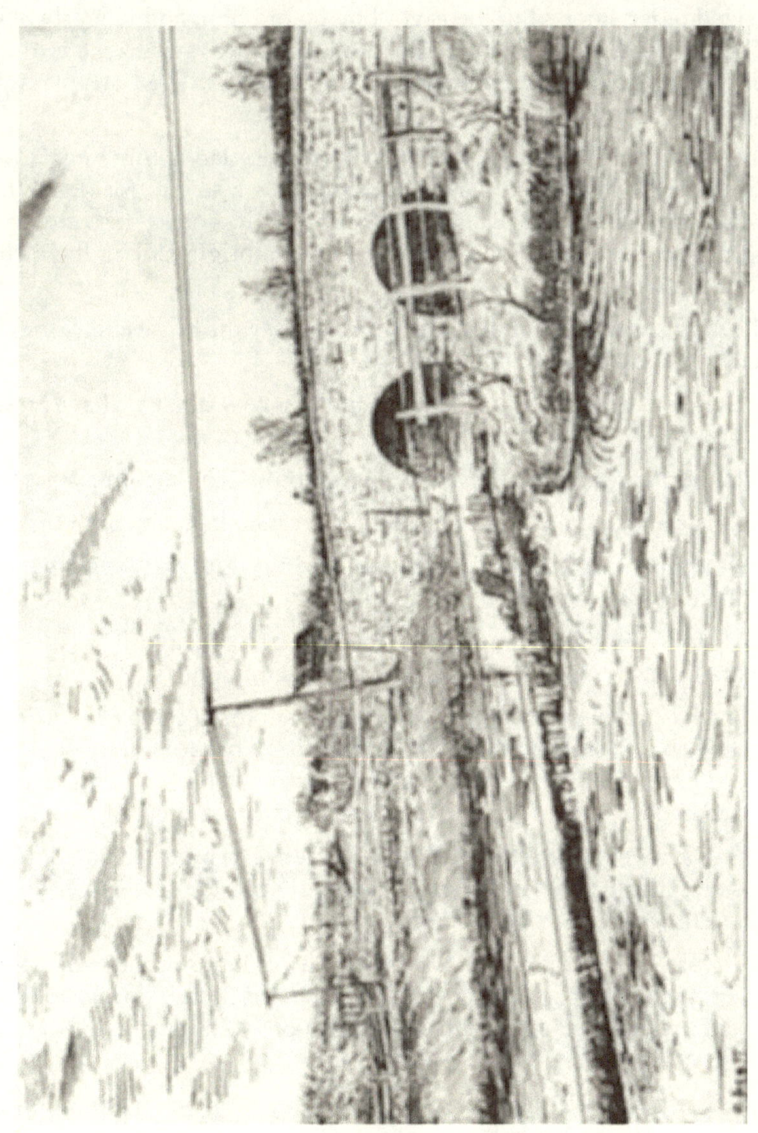

THE STREAM BELOW THE BRIDGE.

The next evening Charlie lost no time in publicly coming out on the Lord's side.

"Brother Oller," said he, "I'm coming. It's decided. I want to be baptized and live a Christian."

The aged elder stooped to the eager boy before him, and tenderly answered, "Well, Charlie, the Lord bless you. The lambs are always welcome in the flock. I hope you will be able to be a valiant soldier for Christ. The Lord bless you, my dear boy."

On the way home that night, Charlie's heart was glad within him. How different it was from the night before. He was soon to be a soldier for Jesus. It did not seem to take long at all to go home, and the hills did not seem so steep, and the night did not seem so dark. He could now see the bright side of life, better than ever before.

While his papa was out at the barn, putting away the horse and carriage, Charlie was talking to his mamma in the house.

"I wish now we had family worship. Mamma, why don't we have family worship, anyhow?"

"Well, I don't know, Charlie, just why we don't," said mamma.

"Well, mamma, papa ought to have it. Other members do, don't they?"

"I guess papa feels a little timid about leading in prayer," said his mamma. "That's all the reason I know."

"Well, I tell you, I'll do my part. I'll take my turn always, if we just can have family worship every day. Won't you ask papa? I think he will."

Sunday was the day for baptism. Two of the brethren came on a visit to examine those to be baptized, before the day for baptism, to learn if they were ready for the holy ordinance, and if they were willing to take the New Testament as the rule of faith and practice, and to walk in harmony with the church.

Charlie's answers were clear and well-defined. The brethren had quite a pleasant visit with him, and they went away feeling that children were very fit subjects for the church, "for of such is the kingdom of heaven."

There were thirteen baptized that day, and a large number of people witnessed the scene. It seemed, as we read about it in the Bible, like apostolic times, as one after another was led down into the stream of water near the bridge, and was there buried in baptism.

When Charlie arose from his knees, while they were yet in the water, the minister, Brother Price, greeted him with a kiss.

After the baptisms, all the people soon went away to their homes, but of all that number, thirteen went away feeling the joy of having entered into a blessed experience, which they had not known before.

That Sunday night the voice of prayer was heard in the home of the Newcomers. Family worship was a daily service there from that time on. Every evening before going to bed the little family would sing a hymn, read a portion of Scripture, and then all kneel down together and pray. And Charlie, true to his promise, and but a boy, yet a *Christian* boy, would always take his turn, in reading, in leading in prayer, and in closing with the Lord's prayer.

CHAPTER VI.

A SATURDAY AT HOME.

After we are once six years old, the most of us have to spend more days, as children, in the school than out of it; and whether Saturday does us very much good, I do not know. The lessons are nearly always not as well prepared on Monday as on other days, for too much time to prepare is about as bad as too little. And then, too, we sometimes forget over Sunday, what we have studied for Monday; but, it is better not to know the lessons on Monday, than to study them on Sunday. Sunday is the Lord's day. The best way of all, however, is to study on Friday and Saturday nights, and then get up a little earlier on Monday morning and review before school time.

Saturday is an off day generally. Girls have a good deal of work to do about the house and boys have a good deal to do about the barn, and sometimes they have to work pretty hard.

Charlie had finished his chores as soon as he could that day and was in the house.

Bessie was very busy fixing her dollies' dresses, for she had five dollies, and they always were so hard on their clothes.

"Boys will be boys," grown up people often say, and Charlie oftentimes would give vent to his boyish nature by just teasing whoever would be teased. He teased Bessie a good deal, and mamma too. He made Dash, his dog, stand in the corner.

He would hide in the evening when his papa came home, until he would hear what he would say upon missing him, then come out from behind the stove, behind the door, or under the table, laughing heartily.

On this particular Saturday, Charlie was through with his work, and while he was helping his mother a good deal in the house, he took to teasing her.

Presently she said, "Charlie, don't do that, for it is not right."

He said nothing to this correction, but went quietly out of the house.

After a little while he came hurriedly in again saying: "Mamma, you said I was doing wrong. I went out to the barn, and crawled up into the hay mow, and I prayed to God to forgive me, for I don't want to do wrong. Will He forgive me, mamma, and will you?"

"Certainly I will forgive you, Charlie, and God will too. Try not to do it any more," answered his mother, as she was wondering if she had not spoken too harshly to her boy.

Some schoolmates came in then and they all went down to the swing under the apple tree, where they had a good time together.

After they all had a turn swinging, they played "catcher" around the house, and "hide and seek," and other games as all children know. At about five o'clock the little visitors all went home.

Some men passed along the road talking very loud and swearing. One of them had been drinking. Charlie and Bessie were looking at their mother as she was doing some evening's work when, in a very thoughtful mood, Charlie said: "Mamma, don't you wish you'd 'a' never had any children?"

"No, Charlie. Why?" said she.

"Well, so many people are so bad,—swearing and getting drunk. Suppose I should turn out that way. Really, I wish I'd die while I'm little."

"So do I," said Bessie.

"Why children, children, you must not talk that way. What would your papa and I do?" said their mother, almost choking on her words, for Charlie had said that a number of times before. "Who made you?" she asked.

"God" they answered.

"Well then," continued their mamma, "you ought to want to live as long as you can, so you could serve Him more. He wants us to do all the good we can."

Both children went into the sitting room, and Charlie got his little account book and figured up how much money he had on interest, and how much the interest was, and counted how much he had in his bank, and then added it all up together. "Bessie" he said, "when I get big I'm going to go to college and pay my own way. See if I don't." Then they played together till they got into a little difficulty, and both ran out to "tell mamma" all about it.

That night Bessie did not go to sleep as soon as usual. 'Twas the same the night before. She seemed troubled. Her mamma thought she was sick. Presently Charlie suggested, "Mamma, I'll bet I know what's the matter with Bessie."

"Well, why don't you tell me, Charlie? I do want to know," said their mamma.

"Bessie wants to join the church," he replied, and his little sister began crying in earnest, and soon cried herself to sleep.

CHAPTER VII.

CHARLIE'S LAST DAYS.

"They who seek the throne of grace
Find that throne in every place;
If we live a life of prayer,
God is present everywhere."

That much dreaded disease, scarlet fever, was the unwelcome visitor to many homes. Bessie was taken by it. While she was ill, Charlie was kept from school, lest other children should take it of him. Often he would steal over to the school house during school hours, and peep in at the window, unobserved, to learn who stood first in his classes. He often watched the spelling class as they stood up in recitation, could tell each pupils' standing, but he himself dared not enter. Those were long, long weeks for Charlie, that Bessie's illness continued. She grew very, very sick. Sometimes it seemed her little life was suspended on a silken thread,—a touch might cause it to snap, and she would be gone forever.

Children converted are children still. Charlie was a boy, although a Christian. Often he came softly into the house, and when he would meet his mamma out of the sick room, he would say, "Don't you wish you had left Bessie be baptized when she wanted to? Suppose she should die." And his poor mother, almost broken down with care for her little girl, was made sick at heart by questions like that.

On the doctor's daily visit Charlie met him at the gate, and would tie his horse for him, and then come with him into the house.

Bessie had lain ill already four weeks. On Tuesday morning the doctor tied his horse himself and came in alone. Charlie was sick. The doctor said to him, "Well, Charlie, you've got it now. Does it scare you?"

"No sir, it don't scare me," he said, "but I hope I won't have to be sick as long as Bessie."

Both were soon hanging in the balances, Bessie in one room, Charlie in another. Charlie wanted to be taken over into Bessie's room, that they both might be sick together.

Day and night the two little patients were closely watched. Charlie was heard making a noise, and they listened to catch the voice. He was suffering great pain but humming the tune in the hymnal, number 118,—not saying the words, but just humming the tune. Often he would ease his pain with this heaven medicine. Twice he was heard to speak distinctly. Once he said "Lord" and again it was "heaven." His lips would move but no sound was heard. The sound was heard in heaven, I suppose. Angels responded to the call of that little child of God. On Friday morning, even before the rays of morning light began to come, his spirit was borne away to be with Jesus in the heavenly land.

In the morning Bessie's papa was sitting by her bedside, looking sadly on the little form of his only child. "Papa," she said "why don't you have the door open in Charlie's room? He'll be so lonely with the door shut." But he made no reply. "Papa," she continued "why do you stay here with me? Take care of Charlie. I'm afraid he's going to die."

Little by little her papa told her then, all about it, and she bathed her fevered pillow with her tears.

The doctor came. He knew the fact without being told, and he sat down and wept.

Sunday, Charlie's little form was laid away to rest in the cemetery at Waynesboro. And at the same time when that sorrowful little company were journeying thither, the little readers of the *Young Disciple* were reading his letter all over the land. The letter is given below, but we will add the date, not the date that it was written, but the date it was read, the date of his burial.

His life is closed in this world, but the influence of it will go on forever. Three dates will tell the story of that life.

Birth, March 31, 1880.
Second Birth, Nov. 27, 1892.
Borne to glory, March 10, 1893.

THE LETTER.

Ringgold, Md.
March 12, 1893.

Our family consists of a dear kind papa and mama, sister Bessie and myself. We all attend church and Sunday-school regularly. Our Sunday school has closed for this season, but will open again in the spring. Papa and mamma and myself are members of the Brethren church. I am twelve years old. I am studying hard to get a good education, and I hope to grow up to be a good man; and when Bro. W. B. Stover goes to India, I feel as though I would like to go out to him in his missionary work. I will close now by asking an interest in the prayers of all the faithful.

CHARLIE MARTIN NEWCOMER.

CHAPTER VIII.

BESSIE.

Four weeks after the close of the life of her little brother, Bessie was able to be out of bed and around about the house once more. With the return of her health grew her anxiety for the church. And in a comparatively short time, Bessie was received into the church by baptism. She was but a mere child, 'tis true, and that is what she is yet. But what is to be done with the children? Is the church not for them? Did Christ not die for them? Does "all the world" exclude children? What does "in" signify, in "bringing up children in the Lord?" What does "come" mean, when the Savior says "Suffer the children to come unto me, and forbid them not"? and what is the meaning of those last three words?

In the Antietam church were a good many good Christians who looked rather doubtfully on the question of children in church. The little girl spoken of in the beginning of chapter five was the first of the children in that congregation to join the church. Others followed, and when Charlie died *in the church*, all were so much rejoiced in his triumphant faith, that the matter was practically no longer a question at all. Very many little Christians now bring blessing to the congregation, and they are often the best in the family to which they may belong.

I questioned Bessie the other day to learn more of her present position, now that she is in the church. I will give to all, the benefit of her good answers.

"How old are you, Bessie?"

"Ten years."

"Some people think ten years is too young to be a member of the church."

"I don't think so."

"Why?"

"Because I think they can do right just as good as older people."

"When were you baptized?"

"Last summer in July."

"How do you know that you love Jesus?"

"Because,—well, I just know it."

"Suppose sometime you should sin, then what?"

"I'd just pray to God to forgive me."

"Are you sure He'd forgive you?"

"Yes sir. The Bible says so."

"How does it come you did not want to wait till you grew up, like many others do?"

"Because I might die and not be saved."

"Suppose at school some of the other scholars tease you, then what?"

"I wouldn't say nothing."

"How long did you want to join the church before last summer?"

"O, I often thought about it. I was under conviction a good while."

"What does it mean to be under conviction?"

"Well,"—and I saw that I had asked a harder question than I thought. After thinking a moment she said, "I just feel like crying all the time."

"What about, Bessie?"

"About things I done wrong."

"What things?"

"O well, little things in school. I'd get angry sometimes, and do wrong things at home, and I was not very good, and-and—I wanted Jesus to forgive me."

"What did you want to be baptized for?"

"For the remission of my sins."

"How did you learn to give that for the reason?"

"I read it in the Bible."

"Are you sure, Bessie, you realize what you're doing?"

"Yes sir."

"How often do you pray?"

"Every evening and often in the day time."

"Do your parents have family worship?"

"Yes sir."

"What part do *you* take?"

"We all read verse about, and then papa and mamma take turn about in leading in prayer, and I always close with the Lord's prayer."

"Didn't any body coax you to join the church?"

"No sir. Charlie and I used to talk about it a good many times when we were by ourselves. That was before either of us was converted."

"Now, then, are you happy, Bessie?"

"Yes sir."

"What are you going to do when you grow up?"

"Be a seamstress, I guess. I'd like to be a missionary if I could."

"Do you realize a change of heart?"

"Yes sir."

"How does it seem?"

"It seems nice."

"But, think well, and tell me several points wherein you are different now from what you were before you became a Christian."

"I feel more happier, and—and—I love Jesus more, and—He loves me more, and—and—I don't want to do any wrong things, and—"

"What would you be willing to do for the Lord?"

"Most anything."

"Suppose the church should ask you to do something you did not want to do?"

"I'd just do it."

"What part of the Bible do you like the best?"

"The New Testament."

"Why?"

"'Cause it tells more about Jesus."

Then Bessie added that she likes that about green pastures, and at once repeated the entire twenty-third psalm.

Children in the church is no late idea. Children, I mean, not babes nor infants. Polycarp, who afterward was bishop of Smyrna, and a martyr, was converted in the year 80, when he was nine years old.

Justin Martyr says many, in early days, became disciples in childhood and were uncorrupted all their lives.

Matthew Henry, whose commentary is so highly regarded by all Bible students, was converted in his eleventh year.

Isaac Watts, whose hymns abound in all hymn books, was converted in his ninth year.

Bro. James Quinter was converted when he was 17 years old, and was called to the ministry at 22, and the present secretary of our General Mission Board was converted at the age of 12. And I doubt not, many among our best workers were converted very early in life.

Yesterday I received a letter from a little child just entered upon her ninth year. She says:—

> "Dear brother Stover, I can answer your letter and say I am
> on the Lord's side. How happy I am, how I would like for you to

have been here when I was baptized. I could hardly wait till the time came. I have got what I have been wishing for two years, and that is to work for the Lord. I go to prayer meeting, and always try to have a verse.

"— — — —."

Children, too often, do not receive all the credit they deserve in some directions. In a little book on the "Conversion of children" the following incident is given. A father was reproving his son for not giving attention to the sermon.

"Father, I heard all the minister said."

"I do not believe it. You were gazing all over the church during the service."

"But, father, I heard all the minister said."

"I cannot believe it, for it seemed to me you hardly looked at the preacher; your eyes were oftener fixed upon the rafters than the pulpit."

"But, father, I did hear all he said, and I can tell it to you."

"Let me hear you try it."

He then began and astonished his father by giving the text, the heads of the sermon, and *much* that was in it.

"I declare, you did hear the sermon after all."

"I told you I did, father, and now I can tell you exactly how many rafters there are in the roof, for I counted every one of them during the sermon!"

The Lord Jesus told Peter to feed His sheep, but before that He said,

"FEED MY LAMBS."

THE END.

Lector House believes that a society develops through a two-fold approach of continuous learning and adaptation, which is derived from the study of classic literary works spread across the historic timeline of literature records. Therefore, we aim at reviving, repairing and redeveloping all those inaccessible or damaged but historically as well as culturally important literature across subjects so that the future generations may have an opportunity to study and learn from past works to embark upon a journey of creating a better future.

This book is a result of an effort made by Lector House towards making a contribution to the preservation and repair of original ancient works which might hold historical significance to the approach of continuous learning across subjects.

HAPPY READING & LEARNING!

LECTOR HOUSE LLP
E-MAIL: info@lectorhouse.com